The YEEHOS Tech-Poetry

My computer mimics My Badminton Players & Gardeners

AUTRICE

Yeeshtdevisingh Hosanee

Droit d'auteur

En vertu de la Convention de Berne, ce livre publié en France est protégé par le droit d'auteure dans tous les pays membres de la Convention de Berne. De plus, la Loi française sur le droit d'auteur, y compris son Ordonnance sur le droit d'auteure international, assure une protection complète tant au niveau local qu'international. Tous droits réservés. Le droit de Yeeshtdevisingh Hosanee d'être identifiée comme auteure de cet ouvrage a été affirmé par elle. Aucune partie de cette publication ne peut être reproduite sous aucune forme, stockée dans un système de récupération, copiée sous aucune forme ou par aucun moyen, électronique, mécanique, photocopie, enregistrement ou autrement transmise sans permission écrite de l'éditeur. "Partie" signifie les couvertures, le contenu, la mise en page, les structures, les codes de programmation (textes) et les images présentées dans ce livre. L'utilisation ou l'altération des images du livre, y compris les changements de couleurs ou de formes, est strictement interdite. À des fins de citation et de référencement, les idées exprimées peuvent être citées et référencées en incluant les détails de publication tels que le nom de l'auteure, le nom de l'éditeur, le titre du livre, le numéro ISBN et la date de publication. Si des phrases complètes sont utilisées dans le texte cité qui incluent les détails de publication, la phrase complète doit être citée. Vous ne devez pas diffuser ce livre sous quelque format que ce soit. Les informations contenues dans ce livre sont fournies à titre de matériel de référence générale et à des fins éducatives uniquement et ne remplacent pas les conseils professionnels. Par conséquent, avant de prendre toute action, à l'exception de la pratique des codes sur papier ou ordinateur, basée sur les exemples ou les informations contenues dans le livre, nous vous encourageons à consulter un professionnel approprié.

L'UTILISATION DES INFORMATIONS CONTENUES DANS CE LIVRE SE FAIT UNIQUEMENT À VOS PROPRES RISQUES

Édition : BoD · Books on Demand GmbH,
In de Tarpen 42, 22848 Norderstedt (Allemagne)

Impression : Libri Plureos GmbH, Friedensallee 273,
22763 Hamburg (Allemagne)

ISBN : 978-2-3225-5833-9

Dépôt legal: Novembre 2024 (Envoyez à la BnF)

A Special Thought For Readers

Dear Readers,

This book is crafted to inspire and nurture digital skills as a holistic part in our society. Computers are our friends in daily life, understanding how we need to communicate with them through our daily use.

Communicating with computers goes beyond mere interaction; it involves understanding how to engage with them in ways that mimic human communication. This reciprocal understanding is crucial for building a harmonious relationship with technology. By learning how computers operate and how they can be instructed to perform tasks, we can avoid potential financial pitfalls and make more cost-effective decisions in our electronic purchases.

Moreover, this knowledge empowers us to create our own software applications, paving the way for innovation and entrepreneurship. By harnessing digital skills, we can transform our ideas into reality, becoming entrepreneurs in our own right and contributing to the digital economy. This book aims to equip readers with the necessary skills and insights to thrive in a world where technology is a constant and ever-evolving presence.

I hope this book serves as a pioneering resource in poetry literature, enhancing cross-skills of digital and social ones.

Thank you for being part of this tech community through your purchase.

Regards,

Y.Hosanee

Table of Contents

1.	The BADMINTON PLAYERS	PG 8
2.	The GARDENERS	PG 10
3.	The COMPUTERS	PG 12
4.	The TOOLS of the BADMINTON PLAYERS & GARDENERS	PG 14
5.	TOOLS and SKILLS of computers	PG 18
6.	The SKILLS of computers	PG 21
7.	The SEQUENTIAL FLOWS of computers	PG 24
8.	The RANDOM FLOWS of computers	PG 27
9.	The REPETITION FLOWS of computers	PG 29
10.	Try ONE TECH-POETRY?	PG 31
11.	Author's BIOGRAPHY	PG 33

TP1.   The BADMINTON PLAYERS

The badminton player, a human,

Have one or two opponents,

as human players too.

A player usually plays the badminton game,

With one or two opponents tame.

In the game court, all take their stance,

Hitting the shuttlecock with a stance,

Back and forth, the game does advance.

With badminton racquet in hand,

they leap and bound,

The shuttlecock, in the air, is found,

A dance of skill, on the ground.

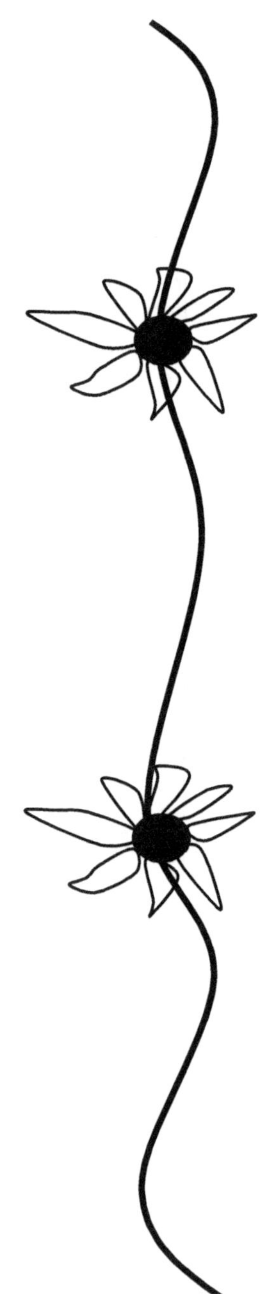

One or two opponents, it does not matter,

The game of badminton, the players will clatter,

With agility and speed, the players will chatter.

The human players, in the game's embrace,

Finds joy and challenge, in this pace and space,

With every hit, the players redefine the race and grace.

TP2.   The GARDENERS

The gardener, a human,

Tends to the garden's game,

With plants and soil, their opponents tame.

In the plot, gardeners take their stance,

Cultivating with careful hands,

Seeds and saplings, they do advance.

With tools in hand, they dig and sow,

The earth, in their care, does grow a dance.

With weeds and pests, it does not matter,

The garden's growth, gardeners will clatter,

With patience and skill, they will chatter.

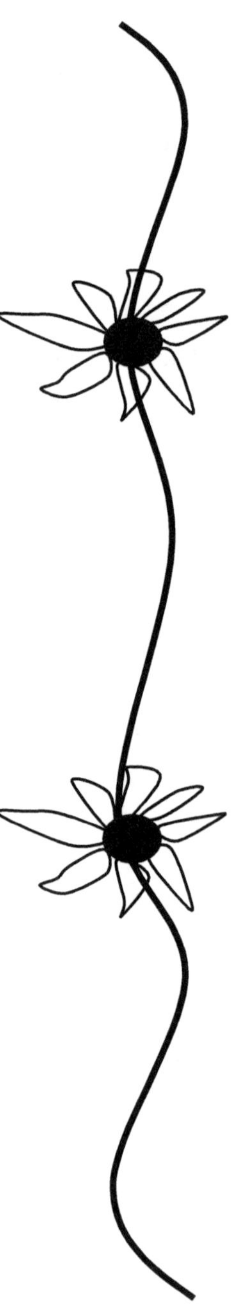

The human gardeners, in nature's embrace,

Finds beauty and purpose, in this space,

With every plant, they enhance the place.

TP3.   The COMPUTERS

The computer, a non-human player,

Lives in human's physical environment,

Unlike objects, computers are chatty actors.

They talk both in a physical and a digital world.

Sometimes acting useful, sometimes nuisance,

To the human world.

With tools in hand, the computers dig and sow,

Their digital world, to talk to the physical world,

Where human exists in a human world.

Nuisance as errors, the computers do not falter,

The digital flows will vary and alter,

To become useful to the human world.

Like badminton players and gardeners,

Computers wield tools and skills to refine,

Correcting errors, intertwining the design,

To redefine their space, joining the cyber line.

So, like badminton players and gardeners,

The computer, in the gaming embrace,

Discovers its role, its digital place,

With every move, it redefines the virtual race,

To meet the physical human world pace,

To make users happy to their grace.

TP4. The TOOLS of the BADMINTON PLAYERS & GARDENERS

Playing badminton in a court,

Looks like a mission for gardening.

The preparedness is lengthy,

The waiting time is not groovy,

A player might end up moody.

For badminton players consciousness,

The sumptuous lengthy preparedness,

Include the headedness of finding equipment tools,

In cleverness for the Badminton racquets, their grip bands
shuttlecocks, proper footwear, clothes as specialness tools.

For the gardeners' consciousness,

The sumptuous lengthy preparedness,

Include the headedness of finding equipment tools,

In cleverness for the trowels, gardening gloves, Hoes

shovels, proper footwear, and clothes as specialness tools.

The skills of the badminton players

Tools are not the only pre-requisites.

For badminton players to ignite

Their motivation for a game fight.

Skills are also part of these pre-requisites,

For the badminton players to hit the shuttlecock,

in the opposite direction to their opponent's position.

Prior to the game, fixing or ensuring,

The racquet's nets are in their positioning,

Are skills to acquire.

During the game, fluctuating

Between hitting the shuttlecock

hard or smooth, to target the pitch,

is a different skill.

Athletic and perception skills,

Are also important to fill.

A badminton player silk,

To become strong, not to quit.

Alike a badminton player,

The gardener is an actor,

Having his own acting skills.

Prior to gardening, cleaning the tools,

to ensure their proper functioning,

are skills to acquire.

During gardening, fluctuating

Between hitting the hoe or trowels,

Hard or smooth, to target his pitch,

Is a different skill.

After a badminton game

Or a gardening, as same,

The player and gardener,

Carefully keep their tools

In their safeguarding tool kits,

For the next situation to spool.

Skills are tamed,

prior, During and after a game

Or a gardening aim.

TP5.   TOOLS and SKILLS of computers

The computers,

like the badminton players,

And the gardener actors,

Are the society's dancers.

They actively participate,

In activities to anticipate,

a predicted output gate.

This gate open doors,

To their individual goals.

A computer's gate,

Is to direct a user mate,

Through its tools and skills veins.

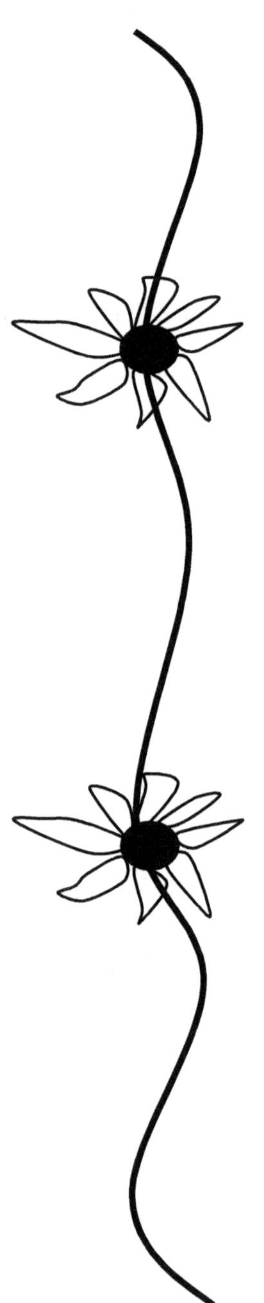

A badminton player's gate,

Is to direct its own weight,

Through its tools and skills veins.

A gardener's gate,

Is to direct the soil's shape,

Through its tools and skills veins.

A computer has tools keen,

As a computer screen,

Keyboard or mouse,

To target its sequential skills.

Likewise, the badminton player,

With tools like racquets or shuttlecocks,

To target his sequential skills.

And the gardener with,

Its trowels, gardening gloves, hoes,

To cultivate and grow sequentially.

TP6.   The SKILLS of computers

Some Skills are sequential,

Apply fundamentally,

To the computers, players

And the gardeners.

Computers follow an

Input-process-output flow,

Sequentially and contextually

In particular shows.

In some other context shows,

An input-output flow is followed.

In other cases, input-output flow

Or input-process-output is glowed,

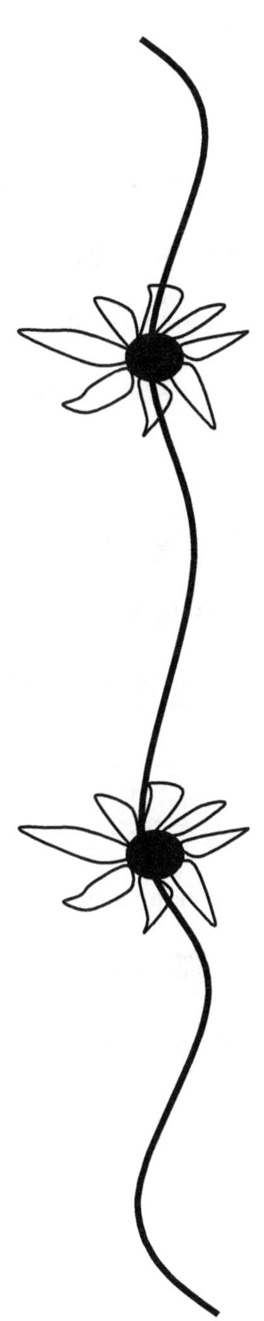

Repeatedly in multiple sequential blows.

In other cases, it is a random blow,

Where input-process-output flows

And input-output sows are,

Not decided in prior.

Forth and back of output-input flows

Or output-input-process-output flows

Can happen repeatedly or randomly.

These scenarios depicted,

Random, sequential and repeated,

Are managed by the skills headed.

inside a computer's bread.

This computer bread consists of,

many cooking skills,

Termed as software.

Like for a badminton player's bread,

And a gardener, their brain cooked their skills,

Sharpened for the tasks ahead.

TP7.   The SEQUENTIAL FLOWS of computers

The input-process-output sequences,

In the digital realm,

can require a computer user to whisper,

to the machine, an English word "girl,"

Yet the computer's task is to twirl,

And transform the word with precision and care,

Into the French language, "fille" to declare.

The computer software, a translator,

Maps "girl" onto "fille", as a coordinator,

Outputs "fille" to the user actor,

Through a tractor output,

the computer screen

The input-process-output thrilled

As input is the English word "girl",

Process is the translation process,

The output is the French word "fille".

In the input-output sequence,

Input is still the English word "girl",

But no translation process occurs,

And the output is the same English word "girl",

To a computer user through a screen.

Sequential flows in computers

Can vary from input-output blow

Or input-process-output glow.

For computers,

The sequential flows are pre-determined.

By the owner of the computer's activities.

For badminton players and gardeners,

The sequential flows are pre-calculated,

By the players or gardeners.

TP8.   The RANDOM FLOWS of computers

A computer user can bestow,

a change in computer flows,

making it random for different contexts.

If two English words are entered to a computer,

"good girl", the input-process-output shooter,

 would twist to input-process-inputs-process-output looter.

English words "good girl" as first input,

The computer software divides the words,

Into two separate words in the first process,

Which become a division step.

The computer software will then,

Use each separate word as two separate inputs,

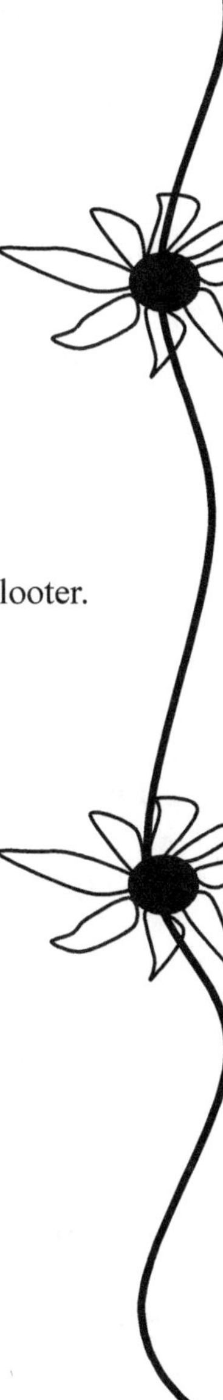

To map them onto singular French word.

"good" will turn into French word "Bonne",

"girl" will turn into French word "Fille".

In the second process, the translation step takes its style.

Once done, "Bonne Fille" appears on the screen,

For the user to see, the transformation keen.

The input-process-output dance varies,

With the inputs' nature, it prepares.

Like the badminton player and the gardener,

Who change their tune with different weather.

For them, the physical world is the key,

Tools and clothes, what they see.

But for a computer, it is the digital scene,

That dictates how it acts, how it has been.

TP9.   The REPETITION FLOWS of computers

The sequential and the random flows,

Can be bent and shaped, as one chose,

To run in one stream or in many,

In repetition, like a song's refrain.

A computer user might desire,

To translate words, more than a pair,

Combining English words with grace,

Into French sentences, a linguistic embrace.

The dance styles between sequential and random,

A conversation's lifeline, on the brim,

Just as badminton players and gardeners blend,

Their skills in both styles, to transcend.

Computers, too, in their digital quest,

Use sequential and random, a dual test,

To perform their tasks with finesse in digital carousels.

TP10.   Try ONE TECH-POETRY?

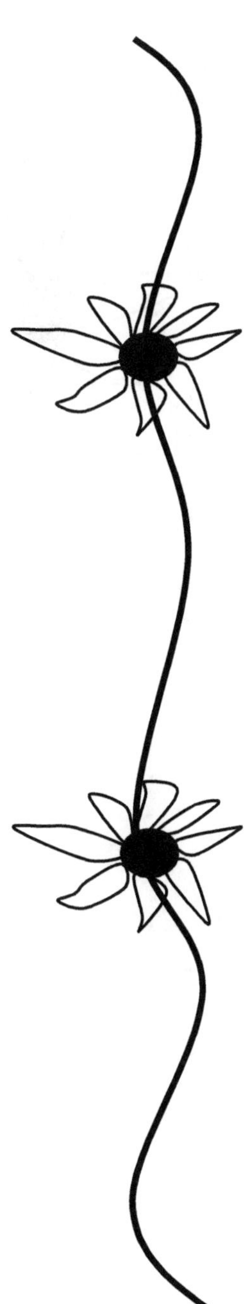

The END!!
The YEEHOS
TECH-POETRY!!

Author's BIOGRAPHY!!

The Author's list of Publications

Table 1 Yeeshtevisingh Hosanee Publication List

	Title	Publication Year	Targeted Age	Book ISBN
1.	PYTHON IN ONE WEEK	2010	20+	Local book in Mauritius (co-author)
2.	An enhanced software tool to aid novices in learning Object Oriented Programmin g (OOP)	2015	20+	Academic Paper
3.	The need to teach object-oriented programmin g in undergradua te courses	2015	20+	Academic Paper

4.	Using different assessment screens to evaluate students' Object-Oriented Programming (OOP) skills	2015	20+	Academic Paper
5.	Is prior knowledge necessary for undergraduate computing courses? A study of courses offered by Mauritian universities	2015	20+	Academic Paper
6.	The implementation of a 2 user proficiency level novice OOP software	2016	20+	Academic Paper

	tool", published in Emergitech2016 conference (Mauritius) – published on			
7.	Teaching English Literacy to Standard One Students: Requirements Determination for Remediation Through ICT, published in Emergitech2016 conference (Mauritius)	2016	20+	Academic Paper
8.	The analysis and the need of ubiquitous learning to engage children in	2018	20+	Academic Paper

	coding-published in 28-30 Nov 2018 conference			
9.	Teaching an IT industry programming language to children of 10 years old-MRIC post-graduate conference 2020	2020	20+	Academic Paper
10.	The Tabular API Testing Framework: used with JMeter and Microsoft Excel VBA	2021	20+	Academic Paper
11.	APRAN PROGRAMMING DANS PYTHON (learn programming in Python, English version)	2021	10+	9789994908653

12.	Learn Python Programming	2022	10+	9789392274787
13.	Learn Java Programming	2022	10+	9789392274770
14.	Machine Learning: The 10 Classifiers In Python	2023	10+	9789392274893
15.	Artificial Intelligence: The 10 Examples In Python	2023	10+	9789392274558
16.	Artificial Intelligence - The Python Chatbot in Australia	2024	10+	9781923020566
17.	Diwali Celebration In Python	2024	8+	9789363555174
18.	Diwali Celebration In Python (French)	2024	8+	9789363553040

| 19. | Mother AI For This Christmas | 2024 | 3+ | Released in Nov 2024 |
| 20. | Mother AI For This Christmas (French) | 2024 | 3+ | Released in Nov 2024 |

Awards

Table 2 Yeeshtdevisingh Hosanee's List of Awards

	Category	Award	Year	Awarder/Location
1.	Drama	Theatre Play in Tamil	2013	Ministry Of Arts, Mauritius
2.	Painting	Certificate Contest	2013-14	Mauritius
3.	Gymnastics	Bronze Medals	2014-14	Mauritius Gymnastics Federation
4.	Research Project	MT180 Mauritius	2019	Campus Numérique Francophone (CNF) de Réduit with AUF Global
5.	Community Work	JCI TOYP 2022	2022	JCI Mauritius
6.	Community Work	Top 30 finalist out of 200 world	2022	JCI TOYP WORLD

		applicatio n For TOYP WORLD 2022		
7.	5+ BOOK	Finalist	2024	American writing Awards (USA)
8.	20+ Book	Winner in Digital Category	2024	International Impact Book Awards (USA)
9.	20+ Book	ABLE Golden Book Award	2024	Author Expo (Australia)
10.	Personality	Global Recognitio n Award USA)	2024	Global Recognition Award USA)

Where TO Find the Author?

Table 3 Yeeshtevisingh Hosanee's contact list

	Where?	Details
11.	Website	www.mycoding.fun
12.	LinkedIn	Yeeshtdevisingh Hosanee
13.	Instagram and Twitter	YEEHOS